Tibetans and Native Americans

FROM THE ROOF OF THE WORLD
TO THE LAND OF ENCHANTMENT

Dedicated to Marcia Keegan 1938 – 2016

Marcia Keegan's legacy is best chronicled in her photography, books, and lifetime of dedication to the beauty of the world that surrounds us. She was committed to documenting the wisdom of the Elders of the Tibetan and Native American ways of life — their respect for all beings, animals, plants, minerals, and spirits. Photography was her paintbrush. Compassion was her religion.

Acknowledgments

Central to both the Tibetan and Native American cultures is the belief that we are all interdependent with each other, that our words and actions have the power to create change, and that the circle of life is unbroken.

I would like to thank the Knowing Foundation and its donors for their generous contributions in making this book of a long-time journey possible:

Jane Bay

Shana Christie

James and Gayle Halperin Foundation

Robin and Roger Himovitz

Satya Kirsh

George Lucas Family Foundation

Evelyn Roisman

Elizabeth Sackler

Ira and Sylvia Seret.

I would like to thank all of my Tibetan and Native American friends for sharing their thoughts, families, images and a way of life that has sustained the legacy of humanity through centuries of change and modernity. I also thank the Office of Tibet and the monks of Drepung Loseling Monastery for all of their prayers.

And most of all I would like to thank my husband, Harmon Houghton, who has been supportive of my work throughout our years together.

— Marcia Keegan

Tibetans and Native Americans

FROM THE ROOF OF THE WORLD TO THE LAND OF ENCHANTMENT

MARCIA KEEGAN

CLEAR LIGHT PUBLISHING
SANTA FE, NEW MEXICO

First Edition
10 9 8 7 6 5 4 3 2 1

Library of Congress Cataloging-in-Publication Data

Names: Keegan, Marcia, author.
Title: From the Roof of the World to the Land of Enchantment : Tibetans and
    Native Americans / Marcia Keegan.
Description: First edition. | Santa Fe, NM : Clear Light Publishing, [2016]
|
    Includes bibliographical references and index.
Identifiers: LCCN 2016016307 | ISBN 9781574161090 (alkaline paper)
Subjects: LCSH: Tibetans--Pictorial works. | Indians of North
    America--Southwest, New--Pictorial works. | Tibetans--Social life and
    customs--Pictorial works. | Indians of North America--Southwest,
    New--Social life and customs--Pictorial works. | Tibet, Plateau
of--Social life and customs--Pictorial works. | Southwest, New--Social life and
    customs--Pictorial works.
Classification: LCC DS731.T56 K44 2016 | DDC 305.895/41--dc23 LC record
available at https://lccn.loc.gov/2016016307

Special thanks to friends who have contributed their talents in editing, producing and designing this book, including Carol O'Shea, Debra Snyderman, Valerie Shepherd, Bo Zaunders, Nan McMillan, Joyce Begay-Foss, and Robert Strautins.

Table of Contents

Foreword
By Harmon Houghton

If a picture is worth one thousand words, then Marcia Keegan's latest book is a chronicle with much to say of the similarities between two ancient cultures that have sustained the human legacy through epochs of change. While our current world view has been shaped by the classic traditions of Greece and Rome, the Renaissance in Europe and the industrial revolution, the Native American and Tibetan Cultures were thriving in a world of isolation from "modernity," maintaining their own traditions handed down through their elders. The Native American emergence stories and world cycles and ceremonies are as alive today as they were in prehistoric times. The Tibetan rituals date back to their root culture of Shang Shung, prior to ten thousand years ago, as the Indigenous culture for the Tibetan plateau. Both cultures evolved with little contact between each other until the 1970s.

When the Dalai Lama first visited North America in 1979, Marcia Keegan was there to arrange the initial meeting between him and the Hopi Elders. The Hopi greeting to the Dalai Lama, "Welcome home," signified a fulfillment of one of their prophesies. The Dalai Lama in response asked, "Where did you get your turquoise?" This signified a recognition of shared values for both cultures. The subsequent dialog explored many common values that reveal the basic human and cultural principles that have guided and sustained the spiritual, economic and governance beliefs of two cultures through centuries of change, and have been codified in a cosmology that respects the dignity of the individual, sacredness of nature, and importance of ceremony as a living tradition. Although the ceremonies and spiritual beliefs differ, the core human values are the same, defined by their land and architecture, people, culture and customs, mountains and spirits, mandalas and sand paintings, ritual dances, petroglyphs and rock art, creation myths, prophesies, and coming together. This book through photographs and text will captivate you and offer a rare glimpse of the heritage of our common human legacy.

Marcia, through her insightful text and photographs, allows you to draw your own conclusions as to what is important, questioning your values in relationship to two ancient and dynamic cultures that have made a contribution to mankind in a non-material manner. The conclusions you draw are your own; the choices you make have their own results for the world that you live in.

Enjoy this book, and ponder the comparison of similarities not only of two ancient cultures but also of the world you live in. It is never finite and always subject to change.

Introduction
By Marcia Keegan

In 1979, a group of Hopi Indians drove all night across the desert toward Los Angeles. When they reached the Wilshire hotel, they were escorted into the presence of someone they had long anticipated meeting. Present were the Hopi Elders Thomas Banyacya (translator for the Hopi), Grandfather David Monongye, Earl Pela, and the driver, Tom Banyacya, Jr.

This meeting of two peoples, greatly separated in terms of geographical distance but bearing unique spiritual messages that have overtones of deep accord, was the fulfillment of a dream for me, and perhaps the fruition of the prophetic traditions of the two peoples.

As a child in Oklahoma and an adult in New Mexico, I have been deeply influenced by the spiritual values of my American Indian friends. Their attunement to nature, reverence for the Earth, and respect for of all things have always seemed to me to be a valuable message for the rest of the world. In the 1970s, while living in the New York area, I became interested in Tibetan Buddhism. Buddhist teachings on compassion and the insight practices of meditation stirred me deeply and seemed, like the beliefs of the American Indians, to offer a profound antidote to the materialist excesses of Western civilization.

As a long-time photojournalist and author of twelve books of photography, I tend to reach for my camera whenever a subject captivates me. In 1979 the Dalai Lama came to the United States for the first time, and I went to a press conference at which he was appearing in New York City. I had never met such a spiritual being. I followed him around the country, photographing him and tape-recording his teachings. As I listened to him and observed his sometimes profound, sometimes lighthearted, and always loving interactions with all those he encountered, I pondered his name, Tenzin Gyatso, which means "Ocean of Wisdom." It struck a chord, stirring up a memory of an old Hopi prophecy I had heard about many times from my friends in the Southwest.

The Hopi prophecy predicts that one day a great spiritual being, a man called Pahana, meaning "salt water," would come to America, and I began to believe that the Dalai Lama was the man the prophesy foretold. I called my Hopi friends who were the tribal Elders and urged them to meet me in Los Angeles to have an audience with His Holiness; I was eager to see how they would react to each other. Hopi Elders Grandfather David Monongye, Thomas Banyacya, and Earl Pela were driven all night in a truck by Tom Banyacya, Jr., to arrive the following morning to greet the Dalai Lama.

On meeting each other, both the Dalai Lama and the Hopi Elders immediately recognized that they had similar facial features, and both commented on the possibility of a common origin. They spent time happily discovering and discussing similar practices and details of their two cultures, based on views and values perhaps sprung from the same source, but then evolving, for centuries, in opposing parts of the world.

The following year, 1980, the Dalai Lama returned to North America, traveling this time to Canada where he gave lectures and met with representatives of many Tibetan and Western groups. Thoroughly captivated by now, I traveled wherever he went, photographing him and taping his lectures.

At the end of the trip, I told the Dalai Lama I would make a book on the trip. I selected 69 photos, combined them with excerpts from his teachings and lectures during the tour, put them together in a book proposal and took it to three different New York publishers in 1981. None of them were interested.

I had already had six books published, so I was surprised that for the first time in my life a book proposal of mine was turned down. I told my husband, Harmon Houghton, that I had promised the Dalai Lama that it would be a book, and I had to keep my word. Moreover, the Dalai Lama was coming back to America around the time of his birthday. The only solution I could see was for my husband and me to start a publishing company and publish the book ourselves.

We rushed headlong into the project. I developed the layout of the book on the living room floor, found a printer who could turn it around quickly and well, and had the book printed, bound and shipped to us posthaste. We gave the first copies of the printed book, *The Dalai Lama's Historic Visit to North America*, warm and glowing from the press, to His Holiness on his birthday, July 6th, 1981. That started our publishing company.

I later redesigned *The Dalai Lama's Historic Visit to North America* as a small book with the same text and a few select pictures called *Ocean of Wisdom*; it has since been published in eleven languages. My husband and I called our publishing company "Clear Light," a phrase with many meanings for me, one of which is an evocative description of the Buddhist mind of enlightenment.

My first six books all focused on American Indian subjects and stories, and the life ways of this culture also continued to be an interest for me, photographically and spiritually. But as my interest in Tibetan Buddhism also grew, and I traveled to Tibet and throughout the Himalayas, I began to see striking resonance between the images I found in Tibetan culture and in American Indian culture.

In Nepal, Bhutan, Ladakh and Sikkim, and in the Tibetan communities in India, I saw images similar to those I had photographed in the Southwest. Without intending to, I found myself making photographs that captured the similarities between the two cultures in visual form. I also continued to arrange for the Dalai Lama and other Tibetan monks to meet my Southwest Indian friends, the Hopi, Navajo and Pueblo Indians, as well as some Iroquois chiefs.

My Indian and Tibetan friends began to discover that they also had similar views on human rights. Indians who had found ways to survive and maintain their culture despite the occupation of their native land by Europeans could sympathize with the struggles of the Tibetans to keep their culture alive in Tibet and in the Tibetan diaspora.

As both groups struggle to preserve their uniqueness and to get their messages out to the world, perhaps their continued friendship will help each one sustain their long-term cultural goals and meet the challenges posed by an increasingly polarized world. The world has much to learn from both of them.

Dalai Lama greets Hopi Elders in California: left to right: Earl Pela, Thomas Banyacya, and Grandfather David Monongye, 1979.

Marcia Keegan and Harmon Houghton present the Dalai Lama with Clear Light Publishers' first book, The Dalai Lama's Historic Visit to North America.

The Hopi Elders give the Dalai Lama corn meal and feather, 1979. Left to right: Grandfather David Monongye, the Dalai Lama, Earl Pela, and Thomas Banyacya.

Land & Architecture

The Pueblo peoples and the Tibetans both dwell in lands of ravishing beauty and demanding climate that are located in similar latitudes halfway around the globe from each other.

The American Southwest, home of the Pueblo and Navajo Indians, and some parts of the Tibetan Plateau that dominates the central portion of Tibet are regions of low rainfall and high altitude that can make daily life challenging. Inhabitants must carefully husband their natural resources and follow strict protocols for agriculture and building in order to live in harmony with their fragile natural environment.

In the Southwestern United States, the ancestors of the Pueblo included the Mogollon in the mountains of New Mexico, Arizona and northern Mexico; the Hohokam of New Mexico; and the Ancestral Pueblo of Chaco Canyon and the Mesa Verde region. These peoples sculpted their homes directly out of the earth, frequently dwelling in caves or in pit houses dug in the ground. Today, the oldest remaining dwellings of the Pueblo peoples are still earth centered, with adobe rooms layered into terraced structures. This building style still endures to varying degrees among the nineteen Pueblos in New Mexico and Hopi in Arizona, but some of the most striking examples are those found at Taos, Acoma, and Laguna Pueblos.

Traditional Tibetan architecture also made use of naturally available materials, sometimes featuring rammed earth or mud over wooden structures. Thick walls were pierced by small windows that kept out the cold and kept the thick structure intact. In areas where trees were more plentiful, elaborate and skillful wooden carving became a key decorative element. Even the lavish paintings on the walls of monasteries were traditionally made with mineral colors pounded from rock or gemstones.

In areas of little rain, roofs might be flat, and, similarly to Pueblo building, the roof of a Tibetan-style structure could become the terrace of the next level. Because of this form of building, some of the monasteries in Tibet and in adjacent regions in

Ladakh or Bhutan strongly resemble the terraced Pueblo dwellings in the Southwestern United States.

In Tibet, the average elevation is 13,000 feet, and, at the turn of the 21st century, rainfall ranged from 3 inches per year up to 35 inches a year in the South, with much of the high central plateau extremely arid. Less than 1% of the land can be cultivated, and the crops that flourish there, such as barley, rapeseed, turnips and cabbage, must be hardy, ripening quickly or enduring spells of prolonged cool weather — though in the wetter south, peaches and apricots grow in warm valleys. Grassland occupies a far larger portion of Tibet than farmland does, and it supports a variety of Tibetan livestock, most notably the yak. Beast of burden, puller of the plough, and source of milk, butter, meat, wool for blankets, clothing, rope and tent covers, and dung for fuel, the yak is the most useful animal in Tibet. The yak's role in Tibetan culture is very similar to that of the buffalo in Indian culture: The animal is held in deep, almost mystical regard, because it has been intrinsic to human survival for so long.

Rainfall in the American Southwest varies across the region, and the climate is changing, but the entire region has been arid for centuries, and the types of crops that can be grown are limited. To insure the proper weather necessary to their crops and their livelihood, the Pueblo people hold many religious ceremonies, both public and private, throughout the year. Through their faithful and conscientious performance of these ceremonies, the cycles of nature are induced to bring forth prosperity and ward off disaster. It is the maintenance of these ceremonies, and with it the harmonious balance of earth, sky, and all the inhabitants between that the Pueblo people regard as their true mission and purpose here on earth. Their vision of life is profoundly cyclic, with beginnings inevitably leading to endings followed by new beginnings.

In Tibet, too, the universe is seen as cyclically coming into being and then ceasing. And like the Pueblo, the peoples of Tibet's high plateaus, mountain valleys and broad grasslands experience nature as spirit. Mountains have resident deities; high peaks, lakes and grottoes are sacred; and all life has a unity of which mankind is a part, not a master.

The architecture of both regions may have been determined by difficult climate, but any hardship imposed by these lands is amply offset by natural beauty. In both places, the soaring mountains and vast arching sky feed a constant sense of proximity to the gods and of unity between earth and heaven. Saturated with the earth's beauty, and with their survival depending on keen awareness of the natural world around them, the peoples of both regions have developed cultures in which the land, sky, rocks, trees, plants and water are all seen as imbued with spirit, enshrining gods and holy beings, vibrant with life and endowed with meaning and mystery.

People who live in such close proximity to nature have a long history of communion with the forces around them, and both Tibetan and Pueblo have intense awareness of nature with its cycles, its challenges, its beauty and its laws. Pueblo stories abound that show the relationships between earth and sky, wind and water, day and night. These forces are personified in gods and nature spirits.

In both cultures, deities and nature spirits dwell in mountains. In Tibet, the *nagas* guard the wealth of waters, and spirits of place protect significant rocks, peaks and caves. Nature deities were honored in the early shamanistic beliefs indigenous to Tibet, but when Buddhism came to Tibet in the seventh century AD, some of the shamanistic beliefs were absorbed into the new religion, and the nature gods were "converted" into Buddhist protective deities. Nature still has a role in Buddhism, though: A key practice is to fully accept impermanence, without resistance or clinging, so nature's constant flux is embraced as inspiration for meditation on the transience of all life.

The interpenetration of the enlightened realms and the earthy material world are symbolized in the Tibetan Buddhist *stupa*, whose form is derived from pre-Buddhist and Buddhist burial mounds. The stupa can be seen as an abstract representation of the meditating Buddha, whose various geometric elements may represent the five elements (the square base representing earth; the round dome, water; the spire, fire; the crescent moon, air; and the finial or dissolving point, space or ether.) The stupa may contain sacred objects such as manuscripts, relics or Buddhist figurines and is a site of pilgrimage, ritual circumambulation, and prayer.

Among the Pueblo people, the *kiva*, a round pit dug into the earth, is used by men of the pueblo for initiation rites and for ceremonies central to the maintenance of tribal customs and continuity, such as war, hunting, and spiritual training. It symbolizes the emergence, through the *sipapu*, from a prior realm into this current one, the fourth world.

Based on both spiritual insight and practical experience, both cultures developed deep-rooted ethics about conservation of natural resources from which the rest of the world could learn. In Tibet and in the United States, the Indigenous peoples face daily struggles getting their messages out and keeping their traditional conservation practices alive.

Hopi village in Arizona.

Leh Palace, Ladakh, India. Ladakh is sometimes called "Little Tibet" because it is home to many Tibetans and their traditional culture."

Acoma Pueblo, New Mexico.

Earthen structures, Leh, Ladakh.

Taos Pueblo, New Mexico, photographed from the water tower in 1971. The water tower does not exist anymore.

Drepung Monastery in Lhasa, Tibet.

Old Laguna Pueblo, New Mexico.

Thikse Monastery in Leh, Ladakh.

Taos Pueblo in winter, New Mexico.

Boudhanath Stupa in Kathmandu, Nepal.

South Kiva in San Ildefonso Pueblo, New Mexico.

People & Culture

Anyone traveling in Tibetan cultural regions or among the Southwest American Indians will see strikingly similar images of faces, dress, daily activities, and implements of daily life. The spindle in the hand of a Tibetan woman and the one being used by a Hopi man look remarkably alike; so are the gestures and attitudes of people herding sheep, buffalo or yaks. A simple fabric, wrapped and tied, may make a child's dress in either culture; horns and animal symbols turn up in ceremonies in both cultures.

The Tibetans and the Southwest American Indians honor the four directions — east, south, west, and north — as well as above and below in their ceremonies. The Navajo hogan always faces east. Tibetan morning prayers feature throwing rice to the four directions, above to the sky and below to the earth. Southwest American Indians throw corn meal in the same directions.

Some similarities in language also exist. For example, the sun and moon are sacred to both cultures, but with a difference. Since they are at opposite ends of the earth, the words for each have opposite meanings. "Dawa" is moon in Tibetan and this same word means sun in the language of the Hopi. "Nyima" is sun in Tibetan and means moon in the language of the Hopi.

Turquoise has similar sacred meaning to both cultures. It blesses the wearer with good luck and protection. The natural gem of Tibet, it has been considered important for health, good fortune, and warding off evil. Turquoise is believed to carry similar protective properties by the Southwest American Indians as well as the ancient Aztec and Inca. Presently, both Tibetans and Southwest American Indians use turquoise primarily as jewelry with the element of protection remaining important for most users.

The Pueblo Indians have been engaged as a sovereign nation in a struggle against foreign domination since the coming of the white man. It has taken much resolute effort to maintain their language, religion, art, and lifeways in the face of the comforts and distractions of modern America. The fact that their cultures have survived for over ten thousand years is a testimony to their endurance and strength.

Since the occupation of the Tibetan nation by China in 1959, Tibetans have been battling to keep their own language and culture alive there. Exiled Tibetan communities struggle to preserve their traditions in the midst of the appeal of the foreign cultures of their varied host countries around the world. The strength and value of Tibetan traditions are revealed not just in images of unchanging Tibet, but in the many images of classic Tibetan culture that can be witnessed everywhere in Tibetan refugee communities in the West.

Tencho Gyatso, the Dalai Lama's niece, from Campaign Tibet in Washington, DC, visits Bandelier National Monument in New Mexico.

Morning prayer: Navajo woman throwing corn meal in the four directions.

Morning prayer: Tibetan woman throwing barley (tsampa) in the four directions.

Yaks in Bhutan. Yaks are a significant part of Tibetan culture as a source of milk for cheese and butter. Butter is used in butter tea and in butter lamp offerings in Buddhist Shrines. Yak outer hair is woven into tent fabric and rope. Soft inner hair is woven into felt. Yak hide is used for boot soles. Yak dung is used as fuel.

Buffalo at Taos Pueblo. The buffalo is a symbol of Native American culture and still honored in Pueblo dance as an important source of food, clothing, and shelter. Some of the money made in Pueblo casinos has been used to purchase herds of buffalo.

Tibetan man spinning wool in Lhasa, Tibet.

Hopi Elder Grandfather David Monongye spinning wool in his home, Old Oraibi, Arizona

Tibetan woman spinning wool in Nepal.

Pearl Sunrise, Navajo, spinning wool in Window Rock, Arizona.

Tibetan woman and girls weaving on upright looms in Lhasa, Tibet.

Navajo woman weaving on an upright loom near Shiprock, New Mexico.

Tibetan man herding sheep.

Navajo man herding sheep.

Tibetan woman winnowing barley.

Ohkay Owingeh (San Juan) Pueblo Woman winnowing corn.

Tibetan woman wearing turquoise and coral jewelry.

Navajo woman, Shirley Francisco, wearing an heirloom turquoise squash blossom necklace and a silver concho belt.

Mountains

The Tibetan Plateau is bounded on the south by the Himalayas, which form a dramatic dividing line between the Eurasian continent and India. This massive range contains more peaks over 25,000 feet than anywhere else on earth, including Mount Everest, the world's highest mountain. At 29,029 feet, Everest, or Chomolungma, ("Goddess Mother of Snows") as Tibetans call it, is so tall that its summit penetrates into the high altitude winds of the jet stream.

The vast mountain chain lies along a geographic fault where the landmass of India pushes up into Asia, crumpling up the Himalayas as a wall between the two regions. The lofty peaks help define the climate both north and south of them, hemming in the cold air of the northern plains and serving as a northern barrier to the monsoon rains in India and Nepal; in other words, a lot of crucial weather patterns really do begin and end in the Himalayas. But despite their significance for weather and geology, the most important function of the Himalayas, from a Tibetan point of view, is that they are the abode of the gods.

The most important mountain, however, is not Everest, but Mt. Kailash, the Tibetans' *axis mundi*, the mystical center of the earth according to Tibetan tradition. Four major rivers, the Brahmaputra, Karnali, Indus and Sutlej, have their source near Kailash, rising from the highest fresh-water lake in the world, Lake Manasarovar. This peak is sacred not only to Tibetan Buddhists, but also to Hindu, Jain, Sikh and Bon faiths, and is the site of pilgrimage by all of these religions.

Tibetan Buddhists see Kailash as the home of Chakrasamvara, or Demchog, a meditation deity known as lord of supreme bliss. Chakrasamvara and his consort Vajravarahi are visualized in union as a symbol of the non-duality of wisdom and bliss. By locating this ideal state of consciousness, the bliss-wisdom of this divine pair, in the sacred mountain, Tibetans envision this lofty peak as a symbol of the indivisible interpenetration of the divine and the material realms. Not only are bliss and wisdom united; so are the sacred vital energy and the material earth into which that energy is concretized.

Kailash is the mountain at the center of the sacred circle of the Tibetan world, and therefore the center of the world mandala, but all mountains have their sacred aspects and local deities, variously honored at shrines throughout Tibet. Some mountains became renowned because they were the site where a great sage or saint spent his or her life in meditation. The cave or hut on the mountain where the sage lived, along with the entire mountain, is revered; it is believed that the place is still filled with the presence of the saint.

For the Indians of the American Southwest, the Rocky Mountains are the backbone of the continent called "Turtle Island." At the base of the spine is the Colorado Plateau, site of the twelve Hopi villages. The Hopi believe the plateau is where the energy of life is stored and held in balance for the entire continent.

The plateau is seen by both Navajo and Hopi as a holy land surrounded by sacred mountains. Navajos and Pueblos, including the Hopi, recognize the sanctity of mountains in four directions. For Hopi and Navajo both, the sacred mountains are Blanca Peak to the east, Mount Taylor in the south, the San Francisco Peaks in the west, and Hesperus Peak in the north.

For the Navajos, each of these mountains is seen as fastened by the gods to the earth by a powerful object such as a bolt of lightning, a great stone knife, a sunbeam, or a rainbow. On each, offerings were placed by the first holy people and sacred beings invited to dwell there.

For the Hopi, the San Francisco peaks are the sacred home of the Kachinas, from which the guardian spirits come down annually to visit Hopi and to which the Hopi make annual pilgrimages. Some of the spirit figures dwelling on the San Francisco peaks are responsible for drawing clouds to the earth, providing moisture for the corn to grow, and are invoked in prayers in ceremonial dances. The activities of the spirits protect the earth, but only if the proper ceremonies are maintained by the Hopi, whose destiny it is to perpetuate these holy homes that keep the earth in balance.

The various pueblos in New Mexico have their own sets of sacred mountains, located in the four directions. The long ranges of the Sangre de Cristo Mountains to the east and the Jemez on the west contain the sacred east and west mountains of the pueblos that lie in the bowl between them. Like the Hopi, the New Mexico Pueblo people also believe that the Kachinas borrow the bodies of human dancers to come down from the mystical mountains to the terrestrial realm.

Many of these sacred mountains have unique roles in the lives of one or several nearby pueblos. Chicoma Mountain, at 11,561 feet the highest in the Jemez range, is sacred to the people of Ohkay Owingeh (San Juan) and Santa Clara. Called Tsikumu or Tsikomo in the Tewa language, it is believed to be the place from which the Santa Clara people emerged into this world.

Taos, the northernmost pueblo in the group between the Sangre de Cristo and the Jemez, holds as sacred its own Taos Mountain with its sacred Blue Lake on top. The lake itself is believed by Taos people to be the hole in the earth through which they emerged into this world. The close of an important initiation ceremony for tribal boys involves a pilgrimage to this lake followed by secret ceremonies that are "off limits" to all non-members.

Thousands of acres of this mountain were taken by Teddy Roosevelt in 1906 and made a part of Carson National Forest. The Taos people were devastated by this, since it meant that hordes of outsiders could at any time trample on the Taos people's most sacred and private altar.

After a long struggle by the tribe and its supporters, the acreage was finally re-turned to the tribe by a landmark court decision in 1970. Tribal members were once again able to control their own natural "sanctuary" and hold their secret ceremonies in peace, without fear of gawking and disruption.

For both Tibetans and Indians, maintaining the mountains as sacred spaces is central to the continuance of their cultures. The mountains are living entities of energy and potential inspiration, not dead rocks to be exploited. As places where the spiritual and material may meet and merge, mountains are worthy of veneration and respect. Those who approach these broad illuminated heights with reverence may find there a place where the boundaries of the limited and quotidian self melt away, to be replaced by a transfiguring sense of unity with all that the universe contains.

Mount Kailash. Photo by Jan Reurink, Sonam Adventures, sonamadventures.com.

Aerial view of Himalayas on a flight from Chengdu to Lhasa, Tibet.

Aerial view of the 11,000-foot peaks of the Sandia Mountains near Albuquerque, New Mexico.

Himalayan mountains near Ladakh, India.

Taos Mountain near Taos, New Mexico. The Taos Pueblo people do a pilgrimage to the top of this mountain once a year, in the fall.

Surrounded by many snow-capped mountains, Yamdrok Yumtso is one of the three largest sacred lakes in Tibet.

Sangre de Cristo Mountains near Santa Fe, New Mexico.

Himalayan mountains of Tibet.

Canyon de Chelly in winter in Navajoland, Arizona.

Field of rapeseed flowers west of Lhasa, Tibet. In the west, canola is the best-known cultivar of rapeseed.

Sweet clover blankets a mountain prairie in northern New Mexico.

Mountains of Tibet with green agricultural fields.

Rocky Mountains of northern New Mexico with grassland.

Tibetan highlands.

San Francisco Peaks, sacred to both Hopi and Navajo people, near Flagstaff, Arizona.

Himalayan mountains near Gangtok, Sikkim.

Mt. Taylor, one of four sacred mountains that mark the four directions and boundaries of the traditional Navajo homeland. Mt. Taylor is the southern boundary and is also sacred to the Acoma, Hopi, Laguna, and Zuni people.

Dry Himalayan mountains with snow peaks.

Dry "badlands" of northern New Mexico.

Mandalas & Sand Paintings

One of the most striking similarities between the cultures of Tibet and the Indians of the Southwest is the use of a cosmic ritual diagram symbolizing a sacred space, often depicted as the four quarters of the world. In Tibet, these diagrams are called mandalas; among the Navajo and Hopi they are sand paintings. In both cultures the diagram often takes the form of a central circle surrounded by a larger circle subdivided into the four directions, sometimes enclosed inside a larger square. The uses of this image vary but often involve integrating the complex play of the energies of the universe into a harmonious whole.

The Tibetan ritual diagram known as the mandala may be sculpted, painted, or made of rice, sand, or other ritual materials. It may be created as a two- or three-dimensional durable object to serve as a symbolic palace or a seat of divinities made inside a place of worship. A mandala may be used as a device to help meditators generate and align particular energies. A mandala could also be created as an impermanent offering — sand, rice, or jewels may be piled up in concentric mandala form, offered, and then disassembled.

Tibetan sand mandalas in particular are often made as part of an extended ritual to invoke certain spiritual energies and deities who, as a result of the prayers and invocations offered, enter into the completed sand mandala and charge the area around it and those present with specific spiritual energies.

Deities may be represented by symbols or more specific images depending on the complexity of the mandala. A typical form of a Tibetan mandala includes the circle, enclosed by a square "palace" that is the abode of the deity, enclosed by a protective ring of fire. The initiate experiences purification through psychically passing through the fire and entering into the lofty spiritual spaces of the inner palace where the deity or deities reside.

The artist or artists creating a sand mandala (usually monks) prepare themselves through meditation and prayer. They consecrate the space in which the mandala will be made, assemble colored sand, clean and level the surface, draw a diagram in chalk, and then carefully fill in the diagram with colored sand. The grains of sand are carefully placed by making them run down either a stick or a very narrow funnel. When the mandala is completed, if it is to be the seat of a particular deity, that deity is invited to enter into it for the purpose of prayers or ceremonies. Mandalas can be created for initiates or for the public. Once the prayer or ceremony is over and the mandala's purpose is completed, it is destroyed to integrate the energies back into the universe and to demonstrate impermanence. The disassembled sand is taken to a river or stream, where it is placed into the moving water to bless the surrounding area.

Because Tibetan mandalas represent mystical energies present in physical space, they are laid out with regard to the six directions. While Westerners are used to the convention that places the east at the right of any map or diagram, the four directions are rotated in the Tibetan mandala to place the east at the bottom. The colors of these directions change depending on the deity or energies being invoked, but the most frequent colors used are red, white, blue, black, yellow, and green.

A similar use of a ritual diagram occurs in Navajo and Hopi culture in the form of the sand painting. Traditional Hopi frequently make sand paintings in the kivas to invite deities for particular ceremonies that would bring blessings to the community. Hopi and Navajo both use small sand paintings made on the earth for blessing a new home or job, a wedding or a newborn child.

A frequent use for sand paintings is to bring about healing. Different clans specialize in healing different diseases and members of those clans would be skilled in making the appropriate sand painting for that disease. After a divination to determine the nature of the illness and the type of diagram that will heal it, the Navajo sand painting will be made directly on the earth and the sick person is invited to enter and sit in the middle of it.

The Navajo construct the healing sand painting in the center of a hogan facing the doorway, which always faces east. To perform the ritual, the medicine man prepares the ground and builds the sand painting by sifting grains of sand from his hand onto the ground. He creates geometric patterns that are symbolic of stories in mythology, usually drawn from some aspect of the creation myths.

The colors most frequently used in Navajo and Hopi sand paintings are red, white, yellow, black, and blue. They are traditionally made from earth. The red is made from red sandstone; white from white sandstone or crushed gypsum; yellow from yellow sandstone or yellow ochre; black from charcoal; and blue from a mixture of charcoal and white sandstone. Sometimes pollen or other plant parts are used as well. Like the Tibetans, the Navajo and Hopi locate east at the bottom of the sand painting. The Navajo sand painting construction begins in the center and is worked from east to west to north to south and back to east, rotating in a clockwise direction.

The Navajo word for sand painting has been translated as "the place where the gods come and go." A sand painting is seen as containing the power of the spirits being invoked. When the painting is finished, the spirits enter in to do their healing work. When the ritual is completed, it is believed that the illness enters into the sand painting, which is then disassembled, destroying the illness with it.

When the ceremony is completed, which must be done in the same day in which the sand painting is constructed, the painting is destroyed. The sand may be put into a wash or a river to return the cosmic energies, so that the blessings from those energies can be available to all beings.

The complete traditional sand painting ritual is usually open only to other Navajo or Hopi people. Those sand paintings that are made as durable art for sale to the public contain only parts of traditional images. This is done to give people from other cultures some idea of this rich spiritual practice without betraying the secrets that have been closely guarded for so long.

The Venerable Losang Samten (called the Mandala Man), came to the US as instructed by the Dalai Lama to demonstrate the meditative art of mandalas. Losang was the first Tibetan to create a mandala in the West. Since then, he has created mandalas around the world. He is seen here working on the Kalachakra mandala.

Completed Kalachakra mandala.

This sand painting represents many of the elements Medicine Men use in healing ceremonies to rebalance the lives of individual Navajos: feathers, directions, sacred plants, animals, birds, and the Yei (spiritual beings). Ceremonies such as the Blessing Way, Feather Way, and Night Way are central to restoring order and harmony to the individual.

73

Tibetan monk, Tsering Namgyal, from the Drepung Loseling Monastery, makes a Dharma Wheel on a mandala.

A young medicine man forms the lightning bolts descending from the wings of a thunderbird, a symbol of inviting the rain to water the arid Southwest. Certain symbols like the thunderbird may be used only during specific times of the year.

75

A Tibetan monk from the Drepung Loseling Monastery gives final touches to the Amitayus Buddha mandala. Amitayus Buddha or Amitabha represents the red fire element, symbolizing long life and pure perception.

The skill and intention of the medicine man, Leslie Francisco, is evident in the careful hand position he uses to release the grains of ground limestone, turquoise, sandstone, and other minerals. A sand painting is never complete: it is always in process. As ceremony, it exists for the time of the ceremony and is then disassembled at sunset.

Mandala of the Compassionate Buddha represented by a lotus flower in the center, signifying the boundless compassion of enlightened beings.

In this sand painting, Pollen Boy is central. The four sacred plants are in the four directions, separated by feathers of the essential earth colors; black, white, blue, green, and brown.

The Dalai Lama dismantling the Kalachakra sand mandala.

Medicine Man Leslie Francisco makes a Yei figure in this sand painting. Each medicine man creates sand paintings according to the be-liefs and traditions of his particular family. The medicine man must be in balance within every aspect of his life as he collects, prepares, and uses the various materials, the plants, and the minerals. If he is following the customs of an actual Chant Way, he is prohibited from varying the details. If the sand painting is for artistic value alone, he may deliberately change details to avoid dishonoring the ritual.

The Amitabha Buddha represents enlightened boundless light and is the Buddha of the Western Pureland

In this sand painting, the Yei Pollen Boy is central with animal horns. He is surrounded by feathers, corn plants, deer, and birds.

Medicine Buddha mandala. Medicine Buddha is the Buddha of healing. He manifests the healing energy of all enlightened beings.

Father Sky, Mother Earth sand painting.

Guhyasamaja mandala. Guhyasamaja is one of the highest tantra deities. Tantra is an ancient tradition that seeks to channel divine energy.

Medicine sand painting of the Yei Pollen Boy in the center of the sun.

Symbols

The predominance of certain symbols in both Tibetan and Southwest American Indian cultures shows another important commonality between the two.

One of these symbols is the swastika. This four-direction symbol is sacred and widely used in cultures throughout the world, from ancient China to the Americas. The meaning of the symbol was universal and positive everywhere, though this fact has become obscured by the Nazis' unfortunately negative and exclusionary misappropriation of it.

The word "swastika" is derived from the Sanskrit *suas*, or auspicious, and *tika*, for mark. This four-direction symbol is found among artifacts in northern India from the time of the beginning of the four-thousand-year old civilization in the Indus Valley to the present day. The shape of the symbol is an elaboration of the universal symmetrical cross. The shape of the cross suggests stable polarity — the solidity of the earth with its balanced dualisms of north and south, east and west, above and below. The four-direction symbol adds four arms, transforming the stable figure of the cross into a symbol suggesting movement and turning. Other explanations call it a symbol for the sun or a rotating "sun wheel." Both these descriptions evoke movement, life, eternity, and creativity.

In Tibet, the four-direction symbol became known as the *norbu zhyi-khyil*, or four-centered jewel. There it is associated with eternal creativity, endless unfolding or becoming. Throughout the Indus Valley region and into Tibet, the symbol appears in both left-handed and right-handed versions on buildings and on household objects. It's a good luck mark, an invocation of blessings, and a reminder of good fortune that comes from being connected to the creativity of the divine.

In the Americas, the four-direction symbol is also ancient and ubiquitous, used by the Indians from the Pacific Northwest to South America. Early examples of the four-direction symbol were found in the 2000-year-old Hopewell Mounds in Ohio. It can be seen in prehistoric Indian sites — on the rock wall at El Morro National Monument in New Mexico and on the sandstone wall at White House Ruin in Canyon de Chelly, Arizona. The symbol is also found in ancient and modern pottery and woven into rugs.

The meaning of the four-direction symbol appears to differ somewhat from tribe to tribe. According to Frank Waters, author of *The Book of the Hopi*, the Hopi people see it as symbolizing the four directions of the Hopi migrations undertaken by the people when, according to their creation story, they emerged from the Third World into the current Fourth World. The center of the symbol is seen as their homeland and represents the navel of the earth, located near Oraibi on Third Mesa of Hopi Pueblo. Waters further suggested that the clockwise rotation symbolizes earth and the counter clockwise rotation symbolizes the sun.

For the Navajo, one representation of the four-direction symbol occurs in the story of the whirling log, a tale that is part of a cycle of healing stories. In this tale, the hero undertakes a mystical journey down the San Juan River inside a hollowed-out log. Where the San Juan River meets the Colorado River, the hero is caught in a whirlpool. The gods rescue him and he sees a whirling cross with Yeis (holy people or spirits) seated on each of the four arms. The Yeis give him the secrets of farming and growing from seed, and the hero returns to his people with this wisdom.

Because of the popularity of the whirling log story, the four-direction symbol was frequently used on Navajo rugs, pottery, and some jewelry, and it was often seen in Navajo petroglyphs until 1940. That year, the Navajo joined the Hopi, the Apache, and the Papago people in a proclamation stating they would no longer use the four-direction symbol "because the ornament, which had been a symbol of friendship among our forefathers for many centuries, has been desecrated recently by another nation of peoples, therefore it is resolved that henceforth from this date on and forever more, our tribes renounce the use of the emblem commonly known today as the swastika — on our blankets, baskets, art objects, sand paintings, and clothing."

The four-direction symbol has represented hope, life, and creativity for many cultures for many thousands of years. Perhaps the association with horror will eventually fade, and the symbol will one day reclaim its original meaning, appearing again in Navajo and Hopi art and artifacts.

Another important symbol for both Tibetans and Southwest American Indians is the gemstone turquoise. Mined for centuries in both regions, the stone is found in only a few places on the earth, in dry areas with acidic, copper-rich soil. The copper gives it a blue color, and if iron is present, it will give the turquoise a greenish hue.

At the historic first meeting between the Dalai Lama and the Hopi Elders, His Holiness asked "Where do you get your turquoise?" The Elders were wearing the turquoise jewelry that has long been prized among the Hopi and other Pueblo people. For Tibetans, turquoise has also long been greatly valued and a frequently used component of jewelry and adornment for both men and women. American Indians believe that turquoise has the power to re-establish the life force, or *chee*, and it is often presented to a patient after a healing ceremony to help restore health. Tibetans also believe that turquoise has healing and other beneficial powers, and is commonly given to a woman by her fiancé in pledge of marriage.

The circle is another significant symbol in both Tibetan and Native American cultures. For Tibetans, the circle represents the cycle of life and time as in the Wheel of Life. For Pueblo Indians, the circle is used as the shape of their spiritual place, or *kiva*, and also used to represent the hole of emergence or *sipapu*. Navajo hogans, or traditional homes, are also circular.

Altars play a deeply meaningful role in both Tibetan and Pueblo Indian cultures. Not only are they found in their monasteries and churches, but are also in private homes. This demonstrates the integration of spirituality into their daily lives.

Nyima Dakpa Rinpoche, Tibetan Bon Master, holds a Hopi rattle with the four-direction symbol.

Ancient sacred symbol for the four directions woven into a Tibetan rug.

Ancient sacred symbol for the four directions woven into a Navajo rug.

Ancient sacred symbol for the four directions (with the sun and moon) painted on a door in Tiger's Nest Monastery in Bhutan.

Ancient sacred symbol for the four directions painted on a Hopi rattle used for dances in Hopi Pueblo, Arizona.

Ancient sacred symbol for the four directions with the sun and moon appliquéed on a woman's vest in Tibet.

Ancient sacred symbol for the four directions carved in sandstone at White House Ruin in Canyon de Chelly, Arizona.

Victory banner made of yak tail hair with a trident, placed on a corner of a temple roof for protection in Ladakh.

Ritual pole with eagle feathers announcing the beginning of a dance in Taos Pueblo, New Mexico.

House protector symbol of yak horns, with an arrow for long life, on the roof of an earthen home in Tibet.

House protector symbol of deer antlers on the roof of an earthen home in Hopi Pueblo.

Tibetan woman with her headdress showing her collection of turquoise. Through the years, women add more pieces of turquoise to their collections on their headdresses, demonstrating the significance of this gemstone in their lives..

Renee Roybal, left, wearing a tablita (type of headdress) for a traditional Pueblo dance, and Bernice Martinez. These women from San Ildefonso Pueblo are wearing their traditional turquoise and coral jewelry, important in dance ritual

The Dharma Wheel or Dharmachakra. This is one of the oldest symbols of Buddhism. The circle represents the perfection of the Dharma, the Buddha's teachings. The 8 spokes represent the Eightfold Path.

Kiva (spiritual place) and Sipapu (place of emergence) in Pueblo Bonito, Chaco Canyon. The circular shape has spiritual significance for Pueblo culture. Chaco Canyon was the center of ancient Pueblo culture from about AD 900 to 1150.

Altar in a Monastery in Nepal.

Altar in Laguna Pueblo in the San Jose Church, New Mexico.

Professor Thupten Norbu (Takster Rinpoche), the Dalai Lama's older brother, beside his private home altar at the Tibetan Buddhist Cutural Center in Bloomington, Indiana.

Private home altar in Jemez Pueblo at Christmas time, New Mexico.

Altar in a Monastery in Ladakh.

Geshe Kalsang Damdul with the Zuni Pueblo artist, Alex Seowtewa. Mr. Seowtewa painted the Shalako and Zuni deities on the altar and walls of this Catholic church at Zuni Pueblo, New Mexico.

Dance

For both Tibetans and Pueblo Indians, dance is a way to bring the gods to earth and to invoke and enter into their superhuman powers.

The Pueblo people dance to align the energies of man with the powers of nature and the plan of the universe. Life is organized around the annual calendar of dances that help to keep the seasons moving, the earth fruitful, and life in balance. Even the social dances, such as the butterfly dance, are petitions for rain, good health, and other blessings.

The drum is like the earth's heartbeat, and the movements of the dance take the dancers to a plane of experience that unites gods, magical beings, and animal spirits with the human participants and audience.

For the more solemn sacred dances, such as the Kachina and Shalako, dancers prepare with long sessions in the kiva, memorizing songs and prayers. They make daily offerings and prepare a special altar. Performing these dances is a grave responsibility, because the dancers are seen as incarnating the energies of the various magical beings witnessed at the dance, such as the Kachinas, or the Shalako, with their different social and ritual roles and symbolism.

In both sacred and social dance, costumes and painted designs have detailed symbolism that is recognized and understood by all participants. Dancers' movements may imitate the movements of the buffalo or the deer in order to invite their spirits to join into the celebration.

Some dances tell stories with instructive and symbolic messages. The Matachina dance, popular in the Pueblos as well as in Mexico, tells the story of Moctezuma, the Aztec ruler, in a version that shows him defeating Hernán Cortés, representing the devil. This tale of good triumphing over evil can take on many meanings, and may have performance variations suited to the events of the time.

Tibetan dance ranges from folk to opera and classical dance to sacred ritual dance. Folk dances include the costumed, miming yak dances that are crowd-pleasing entertainment, but it is the ritual dances that are most akin, in spirit, to Pueblo dance.

Tibetan sacred ritual dance includes two forms, one performed within the monastery for monks and initiates only, and the other in public. Both of these forms of sacred ritual dance have deep symbolism and spiritual messages. A dancer might mime a deer or a skeleton to demonstrate impermanence, and another group of dancers might appear as benevolent or terrifying tantric deities, such as those represented in the Black Hat dance.

The dance itself is a form of meditation, and the making of a mask or a costume to wear in it is a sacred act. The costumes and dance steps may be derived from the imagery of classic Tibetan Buddhist art, or from visions in which the deities appeared to meditating masters.

As with the Pueblo dancers, Tibetan sacred dancers' goal is to merge with the deity being evoked, to portray heightened states of awareness, and to submerge individual consciousness into something more enlightened and more universal. The energies evoked by the dancers benefit not just the performers and the audience, but all beings.

Tibetan Deer Dance in Bhutan.

Deer Dance in San Ildefonso Pueblo, New Mexico,

Masked dancer in a Manifestation of Deities performed by Namgyal monks of Tibet.

Masked dancer in the Matachina Dance in Santa Clara Pueblo, New Mexico.

Tibetan Skeleton Dance in Bhutan.

118

Apache Mountain Spirit Dance in Gallup, New Mexico.

Black Hat Dance, a Tibetan ritual dance performed by Namgyal monks of Tibet.

Comanche Dance in Ohkay Owingeh (San Juan) Pueblo, New Mexico.

Social dance, Tibetan opera in Ladakh.

Social dance, Comanche Dance, San Ildefonso Pueblo, New Mexico.

Ritual Kalachakra Dancer of Tibet.

Harvest Dancer with tablita (headdress) in Santa Clara Pueblo, New Mexico.

Tibetan Yak Dancer.

Buffalo Dancer in San Ildefonso Pueblo, New Mexico.

127

Tibetan Deer Dancer in Bhutan.

Deer Dancers in Ohkay Owingeh (San Juan) Pueblo, New Mexico.

Portraits

Looking at portraits of Tibetans and Southwestern Indians together, one sees that the similarity of facial features is quite remarkable. People of both cultures have brown skin, rounded faces, almond-shaped eyes, straight black hair, full noses, and great smiles. They even share the same non-verbal expressions and movements, for example pointing to a direction or person by simply moving their lips towards it. No words need be said.

These similarities can even cause confusion among the people themselves. One evening during intermission at a Tibetan concert, a Tibetan man started talking to a man from San Ildefonso Pueblo in the Tibetan language. The Pueblo man had to tell his friend that he was Pueblo, not Tibetan.

Underlying the physical looks is a cultural similarity that includes being respectful of all that surrounds them — honoring nature and its bounty, offering prayers of thanks for every occasion, respecting the Elders and most of all cherishing the inner peace that comes from being at one with the world and community they live in. The harmony between nature, water, earth, fire, air and the spirits that surround their communities is expressed in the ceremonies, songs, dances, and seasonal cycles of the earth. Ceremonies for births, rites of passage, marriages, travels, successes, failures, health, and deaths all share a common supported link for individuals and communities.

When added to their strikingly similar physical attributes — skin and hair coloring, the high cheekbones and dark almond eyes — these cultural correspondences tend to reinforce the appearance of their relatedness, and bring into focus the spiritual connections shared by these two geographically separated peoples.

Tibetan woman.

Pueblo woman.

Tibetan elder.

Navajo Elder.

Tibetan Elder.

Navajo Elder.

Rinchen Dharlo of Tibet Fund with Governor Walter Dascheno of Santa Clara Pueblo, New Mexico, and Paljor Thundrup from Project Tibet.

Herman Agoyo of Ohkay Owingeh (San Juan) Pueblo with Lama Gyaltsen of Tibet.

Tibetan woman.

Pueblo woman.

Tibetan girl in Bhutan.

Pueblo girl of San Ildefonso Pueblo, New Mexico.

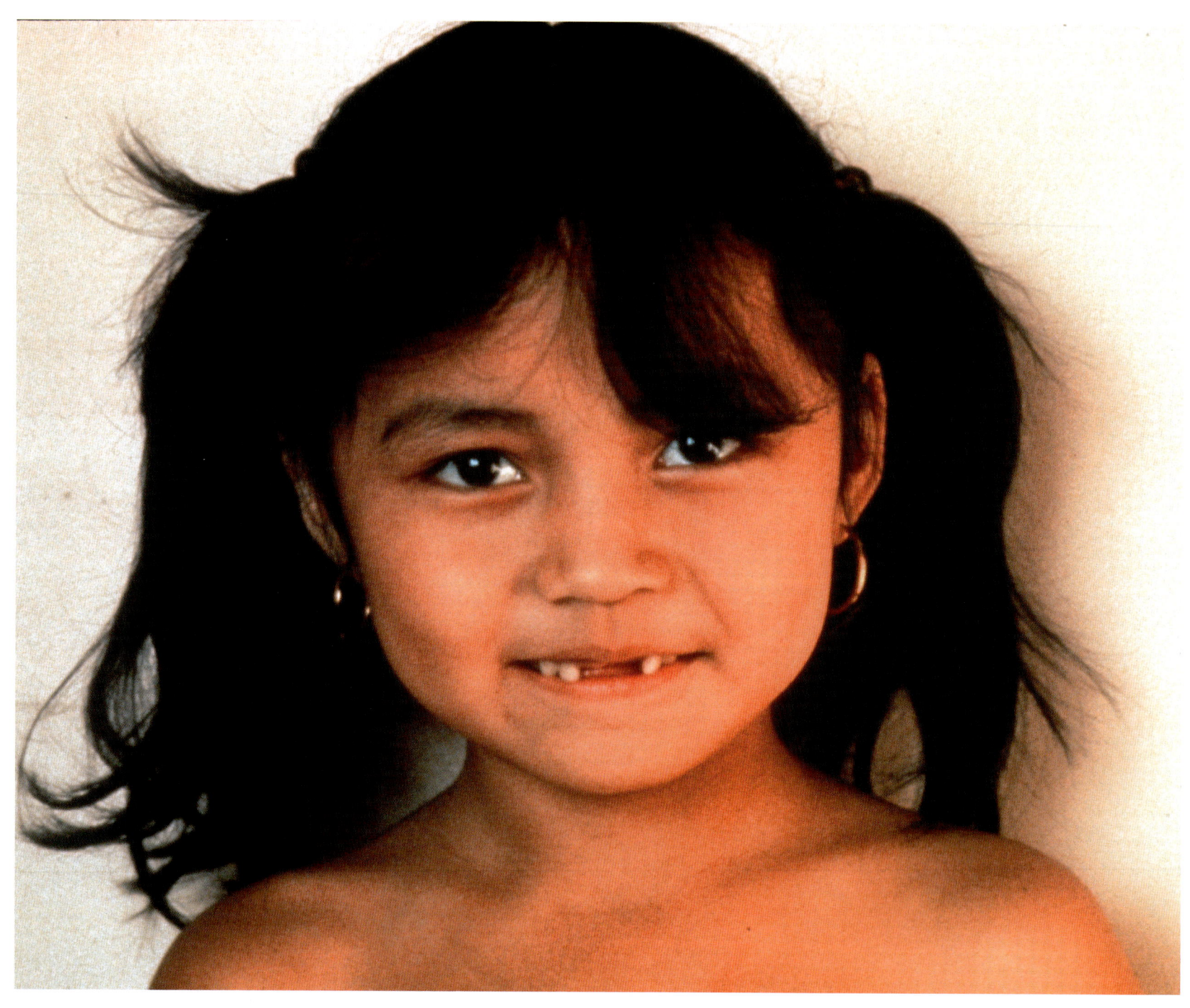

Tibetan girl in Lhasa, Tibet.

Pueblo girl of Santa Clara Pueblo, New Mexico.

Tibetan man in Lhasa, Tibet.

Navajo man in Window Rock, Arizona.

Tibetan girl smiling.

Pueblo girl laughing in San Ildefonso Pueblo, New Mexico.

Tibetan man, a Drepung Loseling monk, visits Kewa (Santo Domingo) Pueblo in New Mexico,
where he meets N.D. Tenorio, who looks like his brother.

N.D. Tenorio from Kewa (Santo Domingo) Pueblo, New Mexico.

Sonam Zoksang (photo coutesy of Sonam Zoksang).

Lorenzo Pino from Tesuque Pueblo.

Petroglyphs

Petroglyphs, or rock-cut line drawings, are found worldwide, but are particularly noteworthy among the Indians of the American Southwest. Petroglyphs are among the earliest forms of representation mankind has created, and have been cut into the rock in both Tibet and in the American Southwest for a very long time. In the Southwest they can be found on cliff and canyon walls, especially near sites that were once ancient villages, now abandoned. Some Southwest rock-cut images may have been made as early as 1000 BC while others were carved in the last century.

The dominant images in Southwestern rock art are those of animals, with humans and deities occasionally portrayed as well. Masks, Kachinas, and abstract symbols or icons such as handprints also appear. A petroglyph in Chaco Canyon may portray an astrological event from the 11th century; others seem devoted to evoking the hunt or a particular dance.

Petroglyphs in Tibet are less well-known, because Tibetan visual art is so diversified that the petroglyphs form only a small portion of that country's artistic patrimony. Most of the petroglyphs come from northern and western Tibet from pre-Buddhist periods (before the 7th Century), many from the Shang Shung kingdom that preceded the Buddhist era, though a few may have been made as late as 1250. Many of the images concern hunting or other animal scenes, and may have had ritual uses designed to bring on a successful chase. They seem connected in content and purpose with the shamanistic Bon religion that predated Buddhism and are remarkably similar in style and content to those found in the American Southwest.

Governor Leon Roybal from San Ildefonso Pueblo explaining the petroglyph to his daughters Sonja and Desiree.

This detail shows a group of animals and anthropomorphs on a rock panel totaling around 140 figures. In the central portion of the image there are two unidentified gourd-shaped objects. At the bottom of the image an anthropomorphic figure brandishes bow and arrow-like objects. Other anthropomorphic figures, ungulates and what may be birds, also grace this rock panel. A magico-ritual theme may be intended here. Probably Pre-Buddhist period. Photo by John V. Bellezza.

Bon teacher Geshe Dhema looking at petroglyphs at Hopi.

Tibetan petroglyph.

Southwestern Indian petroglyph.

In this composition several caprids can be seen. Those with the spiraling horns can most likely be identified as the argali, the largest species of sheep in the world. Pre-Buddhist period. Photo by John V. Bellezza.

Southwestern Indian petroglyph from Monument Valley.

On the surface of this boulder we find a number of intriguing depictions. They include a mounted figure, a standing figure wielding a bow or spear, three dorjes (ritual thunderbolt of Vajrayana), concentric circles and two unidentified bi-circular designs. The bi-circular petrogylphs containing various design elements are the oldest figures on this boulder as indicated by the substantial repatination they have undergone (considerably more than the other figures). Recalling generative eggs, masks and mandalas, it would seem that they represent an important pre-Buddhist cultural theme by virtue of the subsequent carving of the dorjes on the same rock. Photo by John V. Bellezza.

Hopi petroglyphs in Arizona.

This complex hunting scene features around 18 figures including four or five mounted archers and at least eight drong (wild yaks). The vitality and excitement of the hunt is captured here as its participants pursue and fire on their quarry. Pre-Buddhist period. Photo by John V. Bellezza.

Southwestern Indian petroglyphs in Hopi, Arizona.

Tibetan petroglyph.

Southwestern Indian petroglyph..

The Tibetan tradition of rock carving and painting is still quite alive. Even today, travelers may add a painted or carved prayer to a rock on a high pass as thanks for the safe journey.

Three Rivers petroglyph.

Meetings

Twenty years after escaping to India during the Chinese suppression of a Tibetan uprising, the Dalai Lama, the spiritual and temporal leader of Tibet, visited the United States for the first time. And there, in 1979, in a hotel in California, a singular meeting took place between this leader of an ancient spiritual people and four men from another group also struggling to maintain their profound traditional values: the Hopi. The four Hopi present were Earl Pela and Grandfather David Monongye, representing the Hopi chieftains; Thomas Banyacya, interpreter for the Hopi people; and his son Tom, at the wheel of the truck that drove them there.

As they rode through the desert that night to meet him, the four Hopi were aware this could be the realization of one of their own ancient prophesies. According to this legend, Pahana, a spiritual being whose name is derived from their word for salt water, would come to them from the east and help them during a turbulent and dangerous era. Pahana is the Sun Clan brother, the sibling of one of the founders of the Hopi race. The return of this long lost brother would mark the completion of a long period of separation of the two related peoples. The Dalai Lama's Tibetan religious name, Tenzin Gyatso, means "Ocean of Wisdom."

At the hotel, the Hopi presented the Dalai Lama with the auspicious gifts of a prayer feather and corn meal, and their encounter was marked with great friendship. Noting the physical similarities between the Tibetans and the Hopi, the Dalai Lama remarked, "Perhaps in the past we may have come from the same part of the world."

Later that fall, the Dalai Lama met with chiefs of the Iroquois Confederacy at Syracuse, New York, in another instance of this exchange between Eastern and Western worlds. Greeting the Dalai Lama, Chief Leon Shenandoah, the spiritual and temporal leader of the Iroquois nation, said, "Our prophesy says that many things are going to happen to our world — to the plants, all living things, the sun, the moon — if we should ever stop living up to our way of life. Everything has its duty — the sun, moon, clouds, rain, thunder — so that human life is in harmony with nature. So we too, have to live in harmony."

At Syracuse University, the Dalai Lama and the Iroquois chiefs took part in a panel discussion on world religions. At this discussion, a panel member asked the Dalai Lama, "You appear to be a very hopeful man. The question is, what is the basis for our hope for the future? We have had such great tragedies as the holocaust, tragedies of totalitarian nations, tragedies in this country against Native Americans and many others. Yet you appear to be hopeful. What is the basis for your hope?"

The Dalai Lama answered, "Hope is the basis of hope. There is no guarantee, but it's better to hope and try than to not have hope. Our fundamental human way of life is founded on the basis of hope."

The next significant meeting took place the following year in Toronto, Canada. The Dalai Lama met with the Iroquois chiefs and the Hopi Elders for a fire ceremony. Present were Chief Leon Shenandoah of the Iroquois Confederacy, Chief Oren Lyons of the Onondaga Nation, Chief Vincent Johnson of the Onondaga Nation, and the Hopi leader, Thomas Banyacya. Prayers were said for the purpose of peace and harmony on earth. The Dalai Lama shared that the fire ceremony is also a valued tradition in Tibetan Buddhism.

In 1991, the Dalai Lama met with all 19 New Mexico Pueblo tribal leaders at the Santa Fe Indian School in Santa Fe, New Mexico. This was an historic event resulting in a Proclamation that demonstrates Pueblo support for the Dalai Lama and Tibet.

To further bridge the understanding between the two cultures, the Dalai Lama suggested an exchange of American Indian and Tibetan school students. Following up on his suggestion, Marcia Keegan and Harmon Houghton's Ganden Foundation and Friends of Tibet, New Mexico, arranged to send four high school students from the Santa Fe Indian School to the Tibetan Children's Village at the Dalai Lama's school in Dharamsala, India, in 1994. Initially founded as an orphanage for Tibetan refugee children, Tibetan Children's Village is today an exemplary school, teaching Tibetan language and culture as well as a completely modern, westernized curriculum in science, history, math, languages, and liberal arts. The exchange program between the American Indian students and the Tibetan students changed all of their lives.

All participants said when they returned from India that they appreciated their culture and home so much more after meeting Tibetan students who had suffered so deeply. Many of the young Tibetans they met at the Tibetan Children's Village had been smuggled out of Chinese-controlled Tibet. Their parents arranged this in hopes of providing their children with a better life. These very young refugees were grateful for the opportunities offered to them in Tibetan refugee villages in India, but sad to leave their parents whom they thought they might never see again.

One of the American students in the exchange program was William Pacheco from Kewa (Santo Domingo) Pueblo. He went on to college at the University of New Mexico to earn a BA degree in Asian studies and undertook a sponsorship of an orphaned student at the Tibetan Children's Village. Lolita Crespin of Kewa (Santo Domingo) Pueblo married an American Indian man and has a son named Tenzin, named after the Dalai Lama. Teresa Downey of Tesuque Pueblo went to Stanford University and has been involved with Tibetan rights. Yolanda Shoisee of Laguna Pueblo has also been an advocate for the Tibetan people.

William Pacheco is now a teacher at the Santa Fe Indian School. He is currently working to organize another trip for American Indian students to the Tibetan Children's Village in India so that they too can have this life changing experience.

Since those first watershed meetings, there have been numerous occasions when Tibetans and Native Americans have met to share views or speak out on behalf of common interests — to protest genocide, repression, and environmental harm. The insights that they share with one another may help both cultures maintain ancient traditions. The strengths of these deeply spiritual and profoundly ecological traditions can continue to benefit future generations of all peoples.

Upon meeting each other, the people from both cultures seem to have made immediate connections. There have been times when among themselves, there has been confusion as to whether someone was Tibetan or Native American. In many situations, they instantly felt like friends or family, as revealed in the following photographs.

Blessed St. Kateri Tekakwitha

Seven-foot statue of St. Kateri, made by Estella Loretto (right) from Jemez Pueblo, located at the St. Francis Cathedral in Santa Fe, New Mexico. Estella explains the history of St. Kateri to (on the left) Tibetan friends Tsering Tsomo and Tsundue Tsewang and (on the right) Venerable Geshe Wangden Tashi. St. Kateri is the only Native American saint. She was born in the seventeenth century and was canonized in 1980 by the Catholic Church. St. Kateri was a Mohawk Indian woman.

The Dalai Lama meets Hopi Elders Earl Pela, Thomas Banya-cya, and Grandfather David Monongye on his first visit to North America in 1979. They say, "Welcome home." The Dalai Lama says, "Where did you get your turquoise? It's a sacred stone to us also."

Grandfather David Monongye receiving a khata from the Dalai Lama.

Hopi Elders present a feather and cornmeal to the Dalai Lama. Left to right: Grandfather David Monongye, the Dalai Lama, Earl Pela, and Thomas Banyacya.

Iroquois chiefs attending the meeting in Toronto. Left to right: Chief Oren Lyons, Chief Vincent Johnson, Chief Leon Shenandoah, and Hopi Elder Thomas Banycacya.

Dalai Lama (right) meeting with Chief Vincent Johnson and the Iroquois chiefs in 1980 in Toronto.

Chief Leon Shenandoah explains the Iroquois tradition to Ganden Tri Rinpoche in front of the longhouse at the Onondaga Reservation in New York State.

Tibetan scholar Ganden Tri Rinpoche with Grandfather David Monongye, Hopi elder.

Ganden Tri Rinpoche (right) meeting with Paul Bernal, Elder at Taos Pueblo, New Mexico.

Hopi Elders meet Governor Bruce King in his office at the state capitol in Santa Fe, New Mexico, with concerns about climate change in February 1990.

Tibetan Lama Losang Samten visits Thomas Banyacya, Hopi Elder.

PROCLAMATION

OF THE ALL INDIAN PUEBLO COUNCIL OF NEW MEXICO, U.S.A.

WHEREAS, His Holiness, the Dalai Lama is involved in a struggle to place his people and country in an environment free from hypocrisy and religious obstruction and to establish a democratic form of government; and,

WHEREAS, The Pueblo People have endured through centuries of similar oppression: and,

WHEREAS, Because of such experiences, the Pueblo Governors and Officers of the All Indian Pueblo Council understand and share in the trauma and heartache being experienced by his Holiness, the Dalai Lama; and,

WHEREAS, It is the desire of the Governors and the Officers of the All Indian Pueblo Council to encourage his Holiness, the Dalai Lama to continue his struggle against oppressive forces of the world; We do hereby enact the following Proclamation:

Now Therefore Be It Further Resolved, that the Governors of the nineteen Pueblos, each an independent government, and the Executive Officers of the **All Indian Pueblo Council** do hereby proclaim to peoples and nations in the international community, that his Holiness **the Dalai Lama** of Tibet, should be given recognition and authority to settle any and all justifiable claims against all oppressors now occupying his country, and therefore, subduing Tibetans to foreign concepts and controls; and,

Further proclaim that unless native peoples of the world are afforded self-determination and establishment of democratic societies on their terms, the world will suffer great consequences.

Further proclaim that the Dalai Lama will continue to receive the support and encouragement of the Pueblo leadership to whatever extent necessary.

Done this third day of April in the year of our Lord nineteen hundred ninety-one.

James S. Hena
Chairman

Benny Atencio
Vice Chairman

Daniel L. Sanchez
Secretary/Treasurer

STATE OF NEW MEXICO
ALL INDIAN PUEBLO COUNCIL
ALBUQUERQUE, NEW MEXICO

The Dalai Lama meets with Pueblo governors and other tribal members from the 19 New Mexico Pueblos at the Santa Fe Indian School in 1991.

The Dalai Lama greets a visitor at the Santa Fe Indian School.

Spiritual leader of Ohkay Owingeh (San Juan) Pueblo (with Regis Pecos of Cochiti Pueblo) giving the Dalai Lama gifts of traditional turquoise jewelry at the Santa Fe Indian School.

The Dalai Lama with students and dignitaries at the Santa Fe Indian School.

Tibetan monks meet Native American students who traveled to the Tibetan Children's Village in Dharamsala, India (Dalai Lama's government in exile).

Yolanda Shoisee of Laguna Pueblo, William Pacheco of Kewa (Santo Domingo) Pueblo, and Teresa Downey of Tesuque Pueblo, participants in the program in the Tibetan Children's Village, pose with the Tibetan flag. (Missing from photo is Lolita Crespin of Kewa [Santo Domingo] Pueblo.)

Lolita Crespin, the Dalai Lama, Teresa Downey, Yolanda Shoisee, and William Pacheco.

Robert Tenorio (right) of Kewa (Santo Domingo) Pueblo shows his pottery to Doctor of Tibetan medicine, Dr. Yeshi Dhonden.

Dr. Dhonden meets Robert Tenorio in Tenorio's home in Kewa (Santo Domngo) Pueblo.

Tibetan Lama Pema Choegen (left), dressed as a cowboy, talks with a Native American guide, park ranger in the state of Nevada.

Peter Garcia, historian of traditional Pueblo culture of Ohkay Owingeh (San Juan) Pueblo, enjoys meeting Tibetan Buddhist Lama Dorje in Santa Fe, New Mexico.

Tibetan monk visiting a Kewa (Santo Domingo) Pueblo home.

Geshe Tashi Gyaltsen practices using a bow in a Kewa (Santo Domingo) Pueblo home.

Geshe Kalsang Damdul with Gilbert Pacheco from Kewa (Santo Domingo) Pueblo.

Geshe Kalsang Damdul visits children at San Ildefonso Pueblo, left to right: Darlene, Darlynn and Francine Martinez.

Geshe Kalsang Damdul visits Robert Tenerio's home in Kewa (Santo Domingo) Pueblo.

Geshe enjoys coffee with Robert Tenorio's family in Robert's kitchen in Kewa (Santo Domingo) Pueblo. Left to right: Geshe Kalsang Damdul, Robert Tenorio, Pauletta Pacheco, Gilbert Pacheco, and their son, William Pacheco.

Governor Tony Reyna from Taos Pueblo learns techniques for making a mandala.

196

Khamtrul Rinpoche visits Taos Pueblo. He meets Governor Tony Reyna.

Khamtrul Rinpoche also visits the children in Taos Pueblo Day Care with the director, Maria Reyna, the governor's daughter.

Bon Master Nyima Dakpa Rinpoche looking at a petroglyph panel in a Hopi village.

Tibetan Bon teacher exploring Hopi land and finding petroglyphs.

Nyima Dakpa Rinpoche (left) and his assistant, Geshe Dhema (right) meet with Hopi tribal leader in his tribal office.

Desiree Roybal (right), from San Ildefonso Pueblo, reads to 5-year-old Tara Rinpoche.

Tibetan scholar Lobsang Lhalungpa holds Darlene Martinez from San Ildefonso Pueblo.

Desiree Roybal (left) from San Ildefonso Pueblo with Lobsang Lhalungpa's grandchildren.

San Ildefonso Pueblo Elder Julia Roybal and her grandchildren greet the Namgyal monks from India.

Photo of Dalai Lama is placed among Robert Tenorio's own pottery in Tenorio's home in Kewa (Santo Domingo) Pueblo.

Prophecies

According to their various creation myths, the Pueblo peoples came to this world by emerging from a hole in the earth. In these myths, the first people typically left behind a previous world and emerged into the present, or fourth world.

In the creation myths told at Acoma, Kewa (Santo Domingo), Zia and other Keres-language-speaking pueblos, it is two sisters who first emerged, carrying baskets given to them by the Great Spirit, the Creator. In these baskets they found the corn, the animals, the trees, and the mountains of their new home. The sisters brought them to life one by one.

The creation myths of the Hopi and Zuni feature males. In the Zuni myth they are male twins and the Hopi tales center on two brothers. In the Hopi myth, the Creator gave each of two brothers a set of Tiponi, stone tablets that symbolized power, shortly after they emerged. The Great Spirit then sent the elder brother to the East, from which he was to return one day, bearing the tablet as proof of his identity.

The younger brother then led the Hopi on a long stage-by-stage migration to the villages they now occupy. Over many ages, the tale goes, the Hopi moved toward a new land, settled in a new place, built houses, planted crops and harvested them, accumulated the harvest, and, years later, left for a new location. When they departed, they left empty buildings, petroglyphs, and other evidence behind as signs of their former presence there. They believe that, after many centuries of wandering, they arrived in their present homeland, a place foretold to them by the Creator.

A petroglyph on the side of a rock at Oraibi, the third of three Hopi mesas, reveals the story of the Hopi people's emergence into the fourth world, their journey through it, and most importantly, a prophesy about the end of this world. It shows how the eventual transition to the next fifth world will come about and foretells great turbulence at the end of the present era in which many will suffer and die.

According to tradition, the petroglyph depicts the emergence into this world at the far left. The large stick figure is said to represent the Great Spirit and there is a sun marked with a life-giving four-dimensional symbol to his left.

Attached to the first vertical line are two lines leading toward the right, each representing one of the two possible pathways open to the Hopi. The lower is the path of spirituality and tradition—the path given by the Creator. The upper line is the pathway of materialism and modernization—the temptations of foreign ways and culture brought by the newcomers vastly different from the Hopi. If followed, this pathway will eventually lead the Hopi to the complete destruction of their culture, the loss of their power, and the failure of their mission to the world.

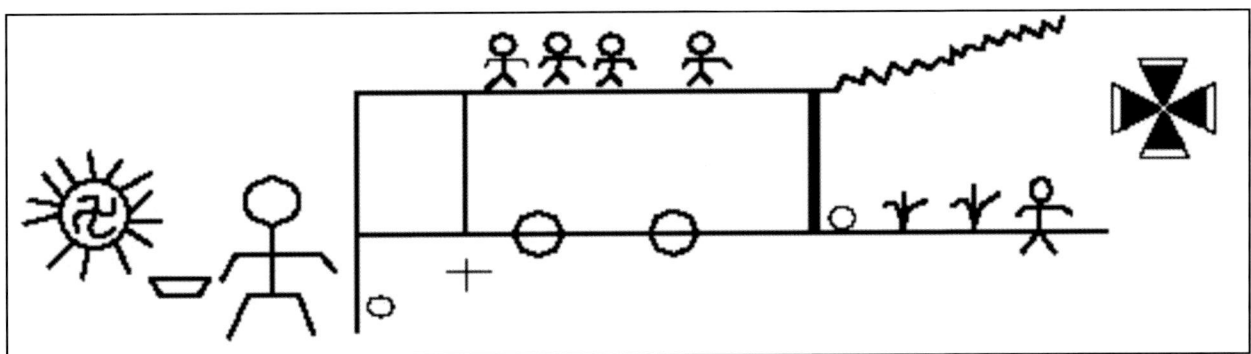

Traditional stories say the two circles represent World Wars I and II. These are to be followed by a third world war, during which those who have followed a materialistic path will be destroyed (the upper line peters off to the right) and only the traditionalists who followed the lower path will survive (the stick figure at the right end of the lower line). This belief that the fourth world will end in disaster, followed by a fifth world, is common to many Pueblo tribes.

The End Time would come about when many Hopi had fallen away from the beliefs taught to them by their forefathers and only a few held onto traditional knowledge and spiritual values brought with them from their original homeland. If those few traditional Hopi were able to maintain the master root of this knowledge, all would be well. If not, then a great natural disaster would befall all the Hopi and the world—possibly wars, earthquakes, or other calamities.

One event that could mark the beginning of the End Time is the mystic return of Pahana, the brother who went toward the East while the other stayed behind to found the Hopi lands. The returning Pahana will bring two helpers, one bearing the sign of the four directions (swastika) and the other, the sign of the Celtic cross (the symbol at the far right of the petroglyph). Pahana, who wears a red hat, will lead a Great Purification that may save the Hopi — and those in the wider world who follow him — from destruction. Peace will reign, the world will be fruitful, and all races will live together as one family. If the Great Purification fails, however, a catastrophic end will follow.

Tibetan prophesy concerns the revelation of Shambala, the land of perfect peace said to be hidden in the Himalayas or hidden from all those who are not yet ready to perceive it. This perfect kingdom is attainable through a journey toward wisdom and compassion, the steps of which grow increasingly more subtle as the goal approaches. The story goes that the kingdom of Shambala will, in the end, be attacked by barbarians who will bring about their own destruction. The victorious king of Shambala will then usher in a reign of perfect peace.

Though the story of Shambala involves, like the Hopi prophesy and like many end-of-the-world legends, an eschatological "final battle" scenario, it is not necessary to imagine this battle taking place on the literal level. It may instead be seen as a kind of inner purification of negatives as one approaches liberation.

Shambala is said to be the source of the Buddhist teaching of Kalachakra, a cycle of meditative practices on the interconnectedness of all life and the cycles of time. The figure of the deity Kalachakra has a black face and on its sides are faces of red, yellow, and white. This might be taken as a symbol of bringing together in peace the four races of white, red, yellow, and black peoples. Coincidentally, the colors of the Hopi four directions are also white, red, yellow, and black.

There is an intriguing line of prophesy attributed to the eighth-century Indian Master Padmasambhava, the saint responsible for bringing tantric Buddhism to Tibet. This much quoted line points to a link between the indigenous people of the Americas and Tibet. It says, "When the iron bird flies and horses run on wheels, the Tibetan people will scatter like ants across the face of the Earth, and the Dharma will come to the land of the red men." Though no actual line stating this can be found in Tibetan Buddhist texts, the line has energized the imaginations of many who have heard it and who are interested in the destinies of both the Tibetans and American Indians — groups that share the challenges of maintaining their ancient and deeply meaningful traditions in the face of multiple threats.

The Dalai Lama has stated that, rather than emphasizing prophesy, Tibetan Buddhists believe in the ability to make positive change and to gain compassion and wisdom.

In 1980, Iroquois Chief Oren Lyons noted he saw spiritual hope in traditional Native Americans after they met the Dalai Lama. Chief Lyons said, "Peace takes effort, and today, in spite of the direction that we see the world moving in, there is also an opposite direction in the awareness of people now beginning to surface. That's where we base our hope, that this may grow. And pilgrimages — for example, the Dalai Lama coming so far to speak on behalf of peace — bring us great hope within our nation. I think this effort must be carried on by individuals and peoples throughout the world. Eventually there will be, we hope, a coming together of all the spiritual people in the world."

Thomas Banyacya, Hopi Elder and translator, shows a cloth diagram of the Hopi prophesy.

The Dalai Lama is presented with a copy of the cloth diagram of the Hopi Prophecy by the Hopi Elders.

The Dalai Lama has said that Tibetans have prophesies too. He has explained that the function of the prophesy is to give the opportunity to change the outcome.

Bon Master Nyima Dakpa Rinpoche talking with a Hopi woman about the ancient petroglyphs on Prophesy Rock in Hopi.

Thomas Banyacya at Prophecy Rock, Hopi, Arizona.